The Church Library

The Church Library

Tips and Tools

BY GLADYS E. SCHEER

THE BETHANY PRESS
St. Louis, Missouri

© 1973 by The Bethany Press

Library of Congress Cataloging in Publication Data

Scheer, Gladys E.   1914-

    The church library.

    Bibliography: p.
    1. Libraries, Church.   I.   Title.
Z675.C5S34   027.6′7   73-10093
ISBN 0-8272-0435-3

Distributed by The G. R. Welch Company, Toronto, Ontario, Canada.

MANUFACTURED IN THE UNITED STATES OF AMERICA

Acknowledgments

It is seldom possible for an individual to know fully all those who, directly and indirectly, have influenced his life and his thinking. Likewise, it is not possible for me to acknowledge all those who have made a contribution, directly or indirectly, to my background out of which this book comes. There are a few, however, to whom I wish to say thank you publicly, at the risk of omitting others who may be as deserving.

To Howard E. Short, editor of The Bethany Press, thank you for asking me to write this book and for being a friend of many years.

To Miss Jeanette Kampen, former assistant editor of The Bethany Press, thank you for guiding the book through the stages of preparation and for great patience in spite of my procrastination.

To Sherman R. Hanson, editor of *The Bethany Guide,* thank you for reading the manuscript and for helpful suggestions as well as kind compliments.

To Mrs. Alfred Grosse, Dallas, Texas; Miss Fern Hunter, Washington, D. C.; and Miss Martha Jones, Nashville, Tennessee, at least one thank you apiece for reading the manuscript and for the good suggestions that hopefully strengthened many of the weak spots.

To both Mrs. Richard Lockett and Miss Debby Marshall, co-workers at Lexington Theological Seminary, who did some of the legwork in order to check information for me, a grateful thank you.

To Roscoe M. Pierson, last but far from least, a more than grateful thank you, not only for much valuable assistance with the manuscript, but also for the many years as co-worker and friend at Lexington Theological Seminary.

For the higher caliber this book has attained, these persons are among those responsible; for errors and omissions, I alone am responsible.

Contents

Introduction

The primary purpose of this book is to help budding church librarians with the "how to" of the various processes of starting and developing a church library as well as promoting its use.

A further purpose of this book is to discuss briefly the "why"—the philosophy—of the church library. Stated simply, the good church library helps, strengthens, and guides the congregation in its mission, education, stewardship, and evangelism—that is, its total ministry. This is said a bit differently in chapter 3 under "Book Selection" in a short discussion of the purposes of the library.

The church librarian is a unique person with a special mission to carry out. The church librarian is, in a real sense, a minister of the church with a responsibility to provide the best possible library resources and then to cultivate within patrons an awareness of those resources—yes, even more, an insatiable hunger for them. It is hoped that this book will help the librarian and the library committee to capture a vision of the possibilities in a church library.

SOME BACKGROUND INFORMATION

Did you know that the library movement in the United States began with parish or church libraries? These early libraries, which began about 1696, were the collections of local clergy who made them available to the people. Eventually from these came public libraries. The early colleges of this country were started by churches for the training of ministers, and their libraries were primarily collections of religious books. Many of these early colleges and their libraries developed into our great universities with their extensive libraries.

The present form of church libraries is dated by some as beginning in 1927 when a layman of the Southern Baptist Convention, Arthur Flake, became concerned about the lack of training and guidance for church librarians. His concept of the library as an organized resource center for eveyone in the congregation led to the present program by the Southern Baptists of training and guidance through field conferences, correspondence, and a quarterly publication that deals with problems of the church library.

At the present time many other denominations have organizations for church libraries and librarians. There is a vast quantity of material available telling how to start, organize, finance, operate, and publicize a church library. Workshops for church librarians are becoming increasingly popular.

Plan of the Book

Although some users might prefer the discussion to begin with books and the guides to their selection, there are some aspects, at least of starting a library, which seem to need consideration first. Therefore, chapter 2 will make suggestions about the physical aspects of the library: location, shelves, card catalog, typewriter, other equipment, and supplies. Once decisions about these are made, full attention can be given to the heart of the library.

Chapters 3 through 6 seem to deal solely with books, with only a hint now and then that there may be things other than books for which a good library is responsible. However, most of the methods suggested for selecting and preparing books will apply to other types of material also. In addition, chapter 7 is devoted to nonbook materials for which the aggressive church library may become responsible.

Illustrations, mainly of catalog cards, are provided in chapter 4. However, because of the limitations of space, there are a number of exceptions and conditions discussed in chapters 4 through 7 that are not illustrated. If you have any questions about these, an examination of the card catalog at the public library would be helpful.

The first two sections in chapter 8 could just as well have been in chapter 6 under "Promotion," but the third section, along with appendix A, is a kind of experiment. Because of the increasing stress of our times and the new ways of meeting and handling, even of anticipating, problems that cause or result in stress, there have been many new applications of possible solutions to those problems. At the present writing, few of these applications are available in book form. If a church library truly has become the help, strength, and guide to the congregation that it is possible for it to be, then its patrons will seek out that library and librarian for ways to cope with the new stresses. The primary purpose for appendix A is to aid the librarian by supplying a list of materials known to be available in areas of such concern. By indicating, possibly in this appendix, which of the material is available locally, probably in the public library, the church librarian will move farther along the path of fulfilling that special mission.

It must be emphasized here at the beginning that there may be more than one way to accomplish the many tasks necessary from the time a book is selected until it is ready for a patron's use. The methods discussed throughout this book will explain one way (occasionally two or three ways, as in the section on classification systems) to do each task. You are free to chose other ways or methods; the important thing is to include each of the steps discussed.

1

Deciding to Plant

WHO STARTS

Often it is the minister, although sometimes it may be one or two concerned lay people, who will suggest that a church and its members really need a library and why doesn't somebody do something about organizing one. The minister, on his own, may assemble some helpful material through the denominational publishing house, and he may also choose the librarian from among the members of his congregation. Or—and this is much to be preferred—he may recommend to the governing body of the congregation that a committee be formed to study the possibility of establishing a church library and to select a librarian and a library committee.

There is a growing tendency for the church library to be lodged in the administration of the church, not just in the education department; that is, the librarian and the library committee are responsible to and report directly to the governing body of the local congregation. The reason for this is based on the fact that the church library should serve the whole church rather than just the church school or the missionary group as it may have originally.

WHO IS RESPONSIBLE

A church with a trained librarian in its membership who is willing to serve as church librarian is indeed fortunate. By adding a small committee, including several young people and/or retired persons to help with the less technical operations of preparing books for circulation, such a church has solved the question of who shall be responsible for the library.

Many churches are not this fortunate and must select a lay person for librarian. An above-average interest in and appreciation of books, a compelling curiosity and interest in finding Christian answers to many of today's challenges, and a willingness to learn simple library procedures are traits desirable in such a person. Additional traits and abilities that are helpful but not paramount include Christian character, consecration, a cooperative spirit, organizational ability, some typing ability, dependability, patience, and definitely an affinity for detail, accuracy, and neatness.

The small committee mentioned above will help with some processes of book preparation, aid in selecting books to be added, be on hand during the hours the library is serviced, publicize the library and its books, determine library policies, and secure the necessary financing.

Two cautions about selecting the librarian: do not choose a person who is already doing effectively one or more other important tasks in the church; do not choose a person who habitually does tasks ineffectively. The position of church librarian, if it is done properly, takes an enormous amount of time and patience and should not be assumed lightly; but, done well, it is one of the most rewarding jobs in the church.

A Specific Library

It has been my privilege to be librarian for Woodland Christian Church in Lexington, Kentucky, since 1954. In 1954 we had 500 books; at the end of 1972 we had 2,500. Each year the Nominating Committee for our Administrative Board asks me to serve as librarian, and this nomination is included on our annual ballot. Although in many areas of library technique our library is far from perfect, comments will be included here and there about our experiences to show that ideal situations are not essential to starting and developing a church library.

At various times from the beginning of Woodland's library we have had library committees, but none of them has been very effective. As a result, at least one of the more important areas has been neglected—publicity. Reading chairmen for the women's groups do very well in getting some of the women to read, but a great many of the members need to be informed about the material available to them from their church library.

You are the person in your church who has just been asked to be the librarian. Although the most you know about libraries probably has come from using the local public library, the thought of having all those lovely, new, clean books to work with is so intriguing and challenging that, in spite of some misgivings, you accept the appointment. Then, almost immediately, you panic; you begin to have second thoughts about your ability to tackle and come out on top of such a demanding assignment. But wait. The committee who chose you did its work well. It secured for you a copy of this book, and we sincerely hope that most of your questions will be answered in the following pages, so read on.

Incidentally, a very helpful tool to supplement this book would be the revised edition of *Outline for Building Vitality in Your Church Library* by Ruth S. Smith. It is available from the Church Library Council publicity chairman, Mrs. Grace K. Fraley, 12204 Atherton Drive, Silver Spring, Maryland 20902. Three supplements to the *Outline* are included: "How to Classify, Catalog, and Prepare Books for Circulation"; "Publishers of Protestant Christian Literature"; and "Church Audiovisual Sources."

2

Starting from Scratch

One of the first important decisions that must be made is where to locate the library. The librarian and the library committee should work together to secure the best possible place. The ideal location for the library is a sizable room of its own as close as possible to the main flow of traffic. This ideal probably is possible only when a new building is being planned or a church is engaging in a remodeling program. Most churches will not be in either group; but there are other possibilities, such as a lounge room, a corner of the social hall, a room off the narthex, or a hallway. It is very important to note that the least desirable spots for the library are the church office, a classroom, or any area not centralized or easily accessible.

If the library *must* be somewhat out-of-the-way, use a pegboard and its shelving for small collections from the library placed in strategic locations, or consider using book trucks to take a selected group of books to the people. On Sunday mornings the selection could be rather general; on meeting nights it could be geared to the needs and interests of the groups involved.

Other important considerations are lighting, heating, ventilation, and attractiveness. If the area is large enough to have study and reading areas, these considerations take on added importance. In this case, tables, chairs, lamps, and other furnishings for the room should be selected from a practical point of view, but also with an eye to a generally attractive appearance.

It would be very desirable to have a small room connected to the library that could be used as a workroom in which books could be prepared for circulation and supplies could be stored. A sink and running water would make such a room even more useful.

Open shelving is much preferable to any other type because it invites browsing, which often results in reading. Adjustable shelves are a distinct advantage because of the various sizes of books. Sections should be no longer than three feet and of heavy enough material to prevent sagging, and solid rather than open backs are sturdier. However, give special consideration to Bro-Dart's Efficiency Shelving—the shelves are forty-eight inches long and are not adjustable, but this shelving does have other advantages including price.[1]

CARD CATALOG

A standard library card catalog should be secured as soon as the library is organized, and it is well, with this piece of equipment, to think BIG. It is true that additional sections can be added as needed, but do consider starting with a section large enough to require supporting legs—a minimum of nine drawers.

TYPEWRITER

A good typewriter with a good ribbon is another very essential piece of equipment. If, or when, a new typewriter is to be purchased, ask the dealer to supply a second platen with a card rail. This is a strip of metal across the length of the platen, but its edges are not tight against the platen. The top edge of all cards can be inserted under the edge of the metal strip, which then holds the top edge of each card securely in place and eliminates the shadowy letters that can appear above the typed material when a regular platen is used. An additional feature of such a platen is that at the bottom edge of the metal strip a small nail can be inserted, against which the left corner of the card is placed as it is slipped under the edge of the strip. In the event a typed card needs additional information added to it, this arrangement will guarantee the card being positioned in the same spacing as before so that additions can be made easily and inconspicuously. The two platens are interchangeable, so when

---

1. Most denominational publishing houses carry a limited selection of supplies for libraries. If the catalog from yours does not include shelving and some of the more permanent furniture, see the list of library supply houses and their addresses in Appendix B, and write for catalogs.

straight typing is to be done the regular platen is used, and when cards are to be typed the card rail platen replaces it.

Other Equipment

As money and space become available, add a desk or table, preferably with drawers; a storage cabinet for supplies; a filing cabinet; a magazine rack; a bulletin board; appropriate storage for pictures, records, filmstrips, and other visual media; and various pieces of projection equipment. *Planning and Furnishing the Church Library* has many suggestions for various situations.[2]

2. Marian S. Johnson, *Planning and Furnishing the Church Library* (Minneapolis: Augsburg Publishing House, 1966).

That Specific Library

Woodland's library is housed in the hall of the education building close to an entrance to the sanctuary. We have four kinds of shelving, all open, and a fifteen-drawer card catalog from a library supply house. We regret that there is no space for tables so that our patrons can have a study area, but any other location in the present facility would take the library too far away from the main flow of traffic we now enjoy. Woodland's library has no work area, let alone workroom, so most of the book ordering and preparation is done in my workroom at home.

Supplies

Another task that needs to be done early—in fact, it can be done before the first books are ordered—is gathering together the necessary supplies. Library supply and equipment companies and their addresses are listed in appendix B, and they will be glad to send catalogs and order forms. The following supplies are necessities:

1. Catalog cards (a minimum of three per book).
2. Book cards (one per book).
3. Book pockets or straps (one per book).
4. Library paste.
5. Items for lettering book spines. These depend on the method you choose. One method requires black india ink, brush, pen

and white ink or electric stylus and white transfer paper. For another method you will need cloth gummed labels and transparent tape (which can be purchased locally). A third method uses black india ink or white ink with pen, or transfer paper (black or white) with electric stylus, and, for paperbacks, felt-tip pens.

6. Transparent plastic coating in a pressurized can.

7. Bookends (a minimum of one for each shelf) unless you plan to make them.

Additional supplies that you may wish to include are: date-due slips, bookplates, overdue reminder forms, alphabet file card guides, shelf labels and holders, ink pad, dating stamp, book repair kit. As you browse through the catalogs from the supply companies, you will want to make note of other items for future purchasing—both supplies and equipment.

Also as you browse, you will discover that there are as many as half a dozen choices each of catalog cards, book cards, and book pockets. You are, of course, free to choose what you think will suit the needs of your library, but here is just a hint about each. Most of the companies offer catalog cards in a card stock that is chemically treated and a bit less expensive than the various rag content cards. We use the medium-weight, unlined, chemically treated cards at Woodland and think they are quite satisfactory. Of the book cards, we have chosen one with a single vertical line near the left edge because this leaves enough room for borrowers' signatures. In the catalogs, near the end of the section on book pockets, several samples of book straps will be shown. We have used these exclusively at Woodland and find them quite adequate. We use the plain ones, partly because it is no trouble to stamp them with our ownership stamp, especially for the difference in price between these and printed ones, and partly because if one side of the strap becomes unusable it can be turned over and reused.

The hints given for these three items will apply as well to the other items: it is not necessary to purchase the most expensive of the choices offered, and it is not necessary to buy one type of item just because you don't know anything different exists. Be a good steward of the funds at your disposal.

3

Preparing the Soil

A church library should live up to its name—it should be a library for the whole church, for everyone associated with a particular congregation. If this is the case, then the financing of such a library should be the responsibility of the whole congregation, and this responsibility can best be assumed by including the library in the church budget. This assures a definite sum of money each year from which to purchase books as well as the supplies necessary to ready those books for circulation. Remember, please, that although this chapter and the next three consider only books, the suggestions apply as well to other media, many of which are discussed in chapter 7.

If additional money is desirable, other sources could be the various church organizations wishing to have books purchased in their areas of interest, or individuals having a special concern for the library. Books given as memorials to loved ones living or deceased are most acceptable and should be encouraged. Gift books should have special bookplates or inscriptions giving the donor's name and the name of the person in whose memory or honor the book is given. A good place for bookplates or inscriptions is on the inside front cover.

One caution: If cast-off books are offered to a library, a legitimate reason for placing or not placing them on the shelves could be based on whether or not the library committee would consider them welcome additions if they had to be purchased from the budget. When castaways are offered to the library, be sure that no strings are attached and be very sure the donor understands that the library committee, guided by its policy statement, will decide which of the books will be added to the library and what will be done with the rest.

A second caution: It must be emphasized, strongly, that money for books or books selected from a prepared list are the only satisfactory gifts, and this should also be made a definite policy of the library. Of course, there are occasional exceptions to this caution. For instance, there may be an individual in the congregation whose personal library contains excellent books that a church library may not have for some reason. In the event the library has an opportunity to secure these as gifts from such an individual, by all means accept them. Be sure to keep the first caution in mind, though, especially if the entire library of such an individual is offered.

Two other possible sources of income are a special-offering Sunday once a year and a modest fine for overdue books. If it is decided to charge such a fine, it would be well to emphasize that this is a contribution to the library rather than a penalty.

Almost from its beginning, Woodland's library has been included in the church budget as a part of the education department. We do occasionally receive money or books from organizations and individuals, but these are our only other sources of income.

Now, what about those simple library procedures that the layman-turned-librarian should be willing to learn? The library committee will help with many of them, but the librarian will have primary responsibility for most of them. Two of the first procedures are selecting and ordering books.

Book Selection

PURPOSES OF LIBRARY

The selection of books will be determined, for the most part, by the purposes of the library. These, of course, vary with each congregation and library, but some ideal purposes would include the enrichment of the program of the church, the curriculum of education, and the lives of the members and their families. More specific purposes within these general ones might be to help the church members grow as persons, to help them understand their own faith, to help them understand people of other cultures and religious beliefs, to help them make moral and ethical decisions, and to aid their spiritual growth—in short, to inspire them, to make them think, to make them laugh, and to broaden their horizons.

With purposes in mind, where, in the great mass of printed material, does one start to select books? Guidelines for evaluating books can be divided into essential considerations and secondary ones.

Essential guidelines include the reliability of the publisher, the qualifications of the author, the up-to-dateness and accurateness of the material, the degree to which it fulfills one or more of the purposes of the library, and the degree to which a book supports Christian ideals and teachings.

Secondary guidelines include the style of writing, the organization of the material, the physical factors (print, paper, binding, illustrations), the book lists and periodical reviews that have included the title.

It should be emphasized that the above guidelines do not sanction censorship. The fact that you do not like a particular point of view or a particular theologian does not give you the right to refuse to add the book to the library so that others may make their own decisions.

It is well to be aware that publishing houses of the various denominations may publish very good books, but differences in theological background may create more problems for the library's readers than they solve. For this reason it is especially important for the librarian to become familiar with all publishers. *Religious Publishing Houses,* a very helpful 1971–72 listing of religious publishers, may be secured—free—by writing to Public Services Department, Vigo County Public Library, 222 North 7th Street, Terre Haute, Indiana 47801. Although the list is not complete and some addresses may be incorrect now, it nevertheless has the most helpful listings and groupings of religious publishing houses that have come to my attention.

SOURCES

Denominational publishing houses. In the beginning the new librarian can rely on the denominational publishing company for catalogs and lists of books from which to make selections. If you live in or near a city in which your denominational publishing house has a bookstore, by all means take advantage of so fortunate a circumstance and browse, at the very least.

The Christian Church (Disciples of Christ) has a Review-by-Mail plan that is available to the church library requesting it. Each quarter, four to six books are sent to the library. These books have been selected by a review committee as good additions to the church library. The librarian and the library committee may take as long as thirty days to examine the books and to decide which to keep. Any books not chosen must be returned within that time; the rest will be billed to the library, presently at a 20 percent discount. With each mailing is included a short discussion of each book, and usually the books are classified by subject and given the appropriate number in the Dewey Decimal Classification System. Write to your own publishing house to inquire about the existence of a similar plan.

Periodicals. Most periodicals coming from denominational publishing houses have a section of book reviews that will be very helpful to all church librarians—experienced as well as new. It would be money well spent to subscribe to those published by your denominational house. Appendix C, "Denominational Services to Libraries," includes addresses. Other religious publications, such as *Christian Century, Christianity Today,* and *Spectrum* (the latter with a new emphasis and frequency since fall, 1972), carry reviews that will be helpful. Also, book reviews found in magazines such as *Time, Newsweek, New York Times Book Review,* and *The Horn Book* often include religious books as well as other books that can be considered for a church library.

Another group of periodicals consists of trade journals published for bookdealers, which, in addition to the great amount of space given to publishers' advertisements, carry articles beamed to sellers but occasionally of interest to church librarians. The manager of a bookstore near you would probably let you look through his copies. You might also be given permission at the public library to look through its book review periodicals and trade journals.

Two other publications to know about (and there may be more) are beamed directly to church librarians; they have helpful articles on all phases of library work, including book reviews. *Media: Library Services Journal* is published quarterly by The Sunday School Board of the Southern Baptist Convention, 127 Ninth Avenue South, Nashville, Tennessee 37234, and is just that—a library services journal. *Church and Synagogue Libraries* is the bimonthly official bulletin of The Church and Synagogue Library Association, P.O. Box 530, Bryn Mawr, Pennsylvania 19010. Membership in the association is open to all interested persons, libraries, and groups. In addition to the bulletin, the association does some publishing and holds an annual conference at which all church librarians are welcome.

Curriculum. Curriculum for the church school and study material for other church groups usually suggest a number of books and other resources as supplementary material, many of which would make good additions to the library. Listing preferences or choosing which to add could well be done in consultation with the teachers.

Book exhibits. Another way to learn about books is to visit the book exhibits provided in connection with church conferences. This will bring to your attention books about which you may not have known otherwise, and it will be an opportunity to handle and look through books about which you have read but whose value to your collection was uncertain.

Usually such book exhibits will also include resources other than books. Many of these may be examined at this time and their value to the total library program determined for purchase immediately or in the future.

Special library week. Many publishing houses encourage, and cooperate in, the observance by church libraries of a special week each year to promote the church library and Christian books. Probably most denominations use National Library Week in the spring of the year for such an emphasis. My own denomination observes Christian Literature Week in the fall of each year.

Denominations that use such a week by making book consignments available to church libraries that wish to order them, provide a very helpful way for the church librarian and the library committee to know about newer books and to examine such books in a leisurely fashion. Of course, the primary purpose of such a consignment is to resell the books to church members and thereby encourage members to read better books or to give them as gifts. Church members often respond to the suggestion that they purchase one or more of these books as gifts to their church library.

Requests. From time to time, library users will suggest books that they think might be good additions to the library. File cards should be made for the consideration file for such books that meet the guidelines established by the library committee so that as money is available these books can be purchased. Almost every request for a book for Woodland's library has been honored if it has met the usual guides of selection and has been in print.

Professional tools. There are several book selection tools that are published for school, public, college, and university libraries for use by professional librarians. These are not particularly recommended for the beginning librarian, who might find them more confusing than helpful, but they can be kept in mind for later use. When that time comes, ask the school or public librarian to show you how to use them. They are: *Book Review Digest, Guide to Reference Books, Library Journal, Cumulative Book Index, Books in Print, Subject Guide to Books in Print,* and *Paperback Books in Print.* Incidentally, *Library Journal* has two issues each year that list "Religious Books to Come," and publishers of religious books do extensive advertising in these issues.

PAPERBACKS

This section on selecting would not be complete without comments on paperbacks. Because of the great number of titles now available in paperback, libraries with small budgets will be able to add many more titles that might otherwise be out of the question for them. For established church libraries and for those with adequate budgets, a new decision may be posed to the church library staff—should paperbacks be purchased and under what circumstances? Here is a suggestion for the library considering the purchase of paperbacks: if the title is one that can be expected to be popular, purchase either the hardcover edition, if one is available, or one or more copies of the paperback edition. However, do not pass up a good book because it is available only in paperback. Most present-day paperbacks are sturdier than the early ones and will wear well even with a number of circulations. Woodland has quite a number of paperbacks, and they seem as popular and wear almost as well as hardcovers.

CONSIDERATION FILE

Most budgets do not allow the purchase of all the desirable books in one fiscal period, so the librarian should develop a consideration file. Each title, with author, publisher and date, price, date the card is prepared, and other pertinent information should be noted on its own file card or 3" X 5" slip. A form in which this material may be shown is found on page 43, figure 3. Arrange these file cards or slips in an order convenient for you— alphabetically by author, alphabetically by title, or in order of preference. Each time books are to be ordered, the file can then be consulted and slips for the desired titles pulled. It is from this file, also, that lists of titles are prepared for those who wish to purchase books for the library. If this file gets too large, periodically weed from it the out-of-date slips. Woodland's consideration file has been a great help in ordering books and suggesting gifts. We usually include a note on each card telling how the title came to our attention and commenting on it if it has been reviewed.

Ordering Records

It is always possible to order books directly from publishers, from book jobbers, or from a local bookstore or department store; however, discounts are often not available from these sources, and this can be important in small budgets. Probably the best place from which to order books, at least at first, is your denominational publishing house. All of these houses supply order forms that can be used whenever books are ordered from them.

If you should want to order books directly from the publishers, an index to publishers' addresses will be found in volume 2, *Titles and Publishers,* of *Books in Print; Cumulative Book Index,* cumulated volumes; and *Paperback Books in Print.* All of these should be available at the public library.

Now that books have been selected, slips have been pulled from the consideration file, and the first order for books has gone to your denominational publishing house, what kind of records must the library keep between the time of ordering and the time of receiving books? If a title is ordered for which there was no slip in the consideration file, make one at the time the book is ordered so that there will be one slip for each title. On each slip or card write the date of the order and from whom the book was ordered (see p. 46, fig. 6). Obviously these cards become an order record file, and all cards or slips can be arranged in the same order as are those in the consideration file. My personal preference is alphabetically by author.

As ordered books begin to arrive, pull the order slip for each title and write on it the date the book is received and its cost (see p. 46, fig. 7). Keep this slip with the book until it has been accessioned and classified (processes explained in the next chapter).

At Woodland, we have found that a second card or slip, which we call a work card, fills a very special need. This card is typed in the same way as the author card (explained in the next chapter), with an additional line on which is given the accession number (in red), the cost, the source, and the date received (see p. 44, fig. 4). From this card and the order card two files can be developed for the workroom area that will save some money and many, many steps, especially if the workroom is in the librarian's home. The work cards are filed alphabetically by the authors' last names. The value of this file increases as the collection increases because it can be checked to be sure that a particular title is not already in the library (the order file also needs to be checked for this purpose), thus avoiding unnecessary duplication of titles and spending of that precious budget. On the few occasions when more than one copy of a title *is* added to the library, accession numbers of the new copies are added to the cards already in the file.

SHELF LIST

The order cards, filed by call numbers, can become a shelf list file (see p. 47, fig. 8). Its value also increases as the library grows because it can be checked as books are added to the sure that a second book is not given the same call number as a previous book.

However, this file has at least two other even more important values. Because the cards are arranged by call numbers, the cards are in the same order as are the books on the shelves—hence the name for the list—and are an inventory of the entire collection as well as a means for determining the strengths and weaknesses of a given division.

As an inventory of the collection, the shelf list helps determine its value for insurance purposes. Therefore, if a workroom area is provided at the church, consider maintaining an additional shelf list in some other place in case of fire, theft, vandalism, etc.

These two sets of cards—author list (work cards) and shelf list (order cards)—are not for the readers' use, of course, but are tools for the librarian and the library staff.

Incidentally, the boxes in which catalog and book cards come make excellent files for these two sets of cards for workroom use. This saves the expense of buying files, and they are easily portable if that should ever be necessary.

4

Planting the Seed

Once a book has been received, what happens next? First, follow the suggestions given at the beginning of the next chapter for opening a book properly and checking the physical correctness of the book. If all pages are accounted for and in proper order, a record of the book should be entered in an accession book. This may be a book for that purpose ordered from your denominational publishing house or a library supply company, or it may be a regular-sized ($8\frac{1}{2}''$ X $11''$) notebook with columns ruled for the book number, author, title, publisher, and cost of the book or name of the donor if it is a gift.

The book number column will start with number 1 and continue consecutively. Each book will have its own number, which should be written in the book in ink on the title page just below the publisher's name, on the top righthand corner inside the back cover, and at the bottom of the secret page you have chosen, which will be the same for all the books in the library. For this page, choose a low number to accommodate small books, such as page 12 or page 15. The book number will also be typed on the top right corner of the book card. If there are two or more copies of a book, the book number will distinguish them from each other, but usually one copy of a title is sufficient. When books are discarded, be sure to rule out their numbers and entries from the accession book.

BUSINESS ENTRY

Another step in processing is to write the business entry in pencil in the book on the first righthand page after the title page, close to the spine and parallel to it. This entry consists of the

date the book was received, the source from which it came
(initials are often used to identify the source, especially if it is
your denominational publishing house), and the cost of the book.
If the book is a gift, the items will be the date received, the word
gift, and the name of the donor.

Ownership Stamp

A library should have a rubber stamp with a minimum of
two lines: the name of the church, and the city and state. This
stamp should be used at three or four places in the book, such as:
the top center of the inside front cover, the back of the title page,
the card pocket or strap, the bottom edge of the book. Other
places than these may be chosen, but at least one place should
be a spot not easily destroyed, and it should be used consistently
in each book.

Classifying

Few church libraries, if any, catalog books—nor should they.
Cataloging involves many more technical procedures than are
necessary for a small collection of books and would be an unnecessary burden to the layman-turned-librarian. Classification
of books, which is one part of cataloging, and probably the
simplest part, is sufficient.

Classifying a book means deciding what the subject of a given
book is. Many books treat two, or even more, subjects in almost
equal proportions. When this is the case, the decision about
where to place the physical book must then be made on the
basis of where it is most logical in relation to the rest of the
books in the library; or where, in accordance with the purposes
of the library, it will best fulfill those purposes.

There are several ways, used singly or in combinations, to
determine the subject of a book. The *title* may be an obvious
indication of the subject, but it often can be misleading; therefore, it is well not to rely on it alone. The *table of contents* or,
if there is none, the *chapter titles* will usually indicate subject
areas. If there is a *preface* in which the author gives his purpose,
aims, and point of view, this will be a reliable source of the
subject or subjects. When these sources fail, it will be necessary
to read portions of the *book itself.* Very occasionally the *book*

jacket blurb may have some helpful hints, but if it and the text of the book are the only sources, it will be well to verify the blurb with samplings from the book itself.

CLASSIFICATION SYSTEMS

Dewey. One of the most important decisions to be made about any library is the classification system that will be used. To state it another way, once the subject matter of a book has been determined, what system will be used to place this book in relation to all the other books presently in the library and to be added in the future? Probably the system known best to most people is the Dewey Decimal Classification System. By far the majority of libraries use it, and this is one advantage for a church library. Many of the book selection aids and some book listings include Dewey numbers, and this would be a definite help. However, in addition to the number, the subject area will also be given so that libraries using a system other than the Dewey system would also be helped to classify that book.

In the Dewey Decimal Classification System, all knowledge is divided into ten basic subject areas, and each area is subdivided again and again and as often as necessary. The ten basic subject areas are numbered from 000 to 900:

000 General works		500 Natural science
100 Philosophy		600 Applied science (Useful arts)
200 Religion		700 Arts and recreation
300 Social sciences		800 Literature
400 Languages		900 History

A second look at this system should bring the realization that the majority of books in a church library would come in the 200s, which would then need to be subdivided quite extensively. It is not possible to develop even one area in detail here, but any church librarian interested in using this system is urged to purchase a copy of the latest edition of *Abridged Decimal Classification and Relative Index* by Melvil Dewey from Forest Press, Inc., 85 Watervelt Avenue, Albany, New York 12206. The tenth edition, published in 1972, is priced at $12.00. Another helpful tool is *Simple Library Cataloging* by Susan Grey Akers. Scarecrow Press, Inc., P.O. Box 656, Metuchen, New Jersey 08840, published the revised fifth edition in 1969 and sells it for $7.50.

In the Dewey system, books for children are usually classified in the same way as all other books, but the letter *J* (for juvenile) is placed at the beginning of the classification number. These books may then be shelved in their proper places in the system, grouped together at the end of the system, or put in some other convenient place—preferably on low shelves the children can reach.

Numbered categories. A system using only broad categories with no subdivisions would be considerably easier for the average layman-turned-librarian. Each category would be given a number, and as books are added in categories not already in the system of a given library, the next number would be assigned to the new category.

Children's books should be considered separately from adult books in this system because young children usually are not too concerned about subject matter as such. Their books could be classified by age groups and be given letter designations to distinguish them from adult books. For older children and youth, a combination of age-group letter and subject-category number might be considered helpful.

In this system no two libraries would necessarily have the same number standing for the same broad category; nor would there probably be any relationship between one category and the categories on either side of it. Such a system might begin like this:

1	Fiction	8	Bible
2	Biography	9	History, Geography
3	Missions	10	Theology
4	Education	11	Worship
5	Evangelism	12	Sermons
6	Devotional	13	Church union
7	Stewardship	14	Music

Whatever main category was added next would be numbered 15.

Classification of books for children and young people would be like this:

A	Preschool	D	Junior high (ages 12, 13, 14)
B	Primary (ages 6, 7, 8)	E	Senior high (ages 15, 16, 17)
C	Junior (ages 9, 10, 11)	F	Young adult

If it were decided to use the combination of letters and numbers, such a system, on the basis of the number designations suggested here, would have classifications such as C8 (books for juniors about the Bible), D2 (biography for junior highs), E6 (devotional books for senior highs), and C14, D14, E14 (three books on music, one each for juniors, junior highs, and senior highs).

Be aware, please, that this is merely a suggested beginning. Each library should develop its own designations for the numbers. One caution: Be sure to *keep an accurate record* of even so simple a system as this one—if for no other reason than to aid a future librarian.[1]

Union. A third system that might be considered is the Union Theological Seminary Library Classification System developed by Julia Pettee. In 1909 Union Theological Seminary in New York City asked Miss Pettee to complete a system for classifying the books of a theological library which she had begun in 1907. A mimeographed listing in 1924 was the first form of this new system, followed by a revised and enlarged edition in 1939. Since then, supplements have been issued periodically by the cataloging staff of Union, with a cumulated edition in 1957. A new edition was published in 1969.

An oversimplified explanation of this system is that in it every field of knowledge is related to Christian theology in a systematic and logical way. Four very broad areas constitute the first major divisions: (1) philology and literature, including the Bible and Christian literature; (2) history—general, church, doctrinal, missions, comparative religions; (3) systematic theology including also the sciences, mathematics, and philosophy; (4) practical theology including sociology, education, the church, its constitution, orders, and ministry.

Each field of knowledge in this system starts with the general and proceeds to the specific. Each subject is given a two-letter, and occasionally a three-letter, designation to which can be added one, two, or more numbers when it becomes necessary or desirable to have subdivisions.

A thoughtful perusal of the following skeleton schedule will shows its logical sequence and its advantage for a church library.

1. A fuller discussion of this method can be found in Erwin E. John, *The Key to a Successful Church Library* (Minneapolis: Augsburg Publishing House, 1958), pp. 7–9.

It is also recommended to ministers for use with their personal collections of books.

A   General encyclopedias, reference books, etc.
B   Languages, literature including fiction
C   Whole Bible
D   Old Testament
E   Apocryphal literature and Judaism
F   New Testament
G   Christian literature
H   General history
I   General church history
J   General history of doctrine
K   General denominational history
L   and M   History by country, both church and political
N   Missions
O   Comparative religion
P   Sciences including psychology
Q   Philosophy and ethics
R   Systematic Christian theology
S   Sociology
T   Education
U   Church: constitution, orders, ministry, law, worship
V   Music and hymnology
W   Practical church work
X   Religious and moral life, devotional literature
Y   Fine arts, practical arts, medicine
Z   Polygraphy and miscellaneous special collections

The first main subdivision of each category is made by adding a second letter to those given above. This means that each of the areas can have as many as twenty-six subdivisions. If further divisions are needed, one or more numbers can be added to the double letters. For instance, *F* is New Testament, *FK* is Synoptic Gospels as a whole, *FK5* is Matthew, *FK58* is commentaries on Matthew, *FK59 is commentaries on special verses in Matthew; FK6* is Mark, *FK7* is Luke, and these are also further divided in the same way as Matthew. In education, which is *T*, *TM* is church school, *TM45* is kindergarten and elementary, *TM45.5* is primary and junior, *TM46.3* is intermediate, senior, and adolescent classes, *TM46.5* is young people and adults.

Children's books have their place in the education section, with some grouped by subject and the rest by age level; therefore, the classification number for all books for children will begin with the letter *T*, although not all *T* books are for children. Those that are for children may be taken out of their places and shelved on lower shelves the children can reach.

A copy of the complete schedule may be obtained from Union Theological Seminary, Broadway at 120th Street, New York, New York 10027, for about $15.00. Woodland's library is classified by an adaptation of the Union system.

Call Number

CLASSIFICATION NUMBER

Whichever system of classification has been chosen, the classification number assigned to a given book becomes the first line of the call number for that book.

BOOK NUMBER

The second line of the call number is known as the book number, and it is used to distinguish books within a subject area from one another. A simple way to do this is to use the first two or three letters of the author's last name.

The professional way to establish the second line of the call number is to use the *Cutter-Sanborn Three-Figure Author Table* (Swanson-Swift Revision, 1969), which can be obtained from H. R. Huntting Company, 300 Burnett Road, Chicopee Falls, Massachusetts 01020, for $10.00. This table combines the first letter of the author's last name with three predetermined numbers. An explanation of how to use the table is included with it and one can soon become proficient in using it. However, if you choose to use this table and have trouble understanding it, the cataloger at the public library will probably be glad to help you with it.

There are at least two advantages to using the Cutter-Sanborn table. The first is due to the fact that the mind has less trouble remembering an initial and three numbers than it has remembering a series of two or three letters (plus the classification number), particularly with names that have variant spelling. Take this book as an example: many people would look for it under *She* and not find it because it would be under *Sch;* but if they were to look for it under *S315* (found on the card in the card catalog), there would be no problem.

The second advantage will not be as evident while the collection is small, but eventually there will come the day when a book by another Jones (or Smith or Lowell or Phillips) will be received in the same subject area as the first book by Jones (or Johnson or Richards or Richardson). If it has been decided to use the first three letters, some other way will need to be devised to show readers the difference between the two Joneses; but if the Cutter-Sanborn table is being used, it has prepared for this situation by allowing four number combinations for the name Jones. Or in the case of Richards and Richardson, the first three letters would not do the job, but in the table there are three possibilities for Richard, six for Richards, and six for Richardson. We use the Cutter-Sanborn table at Woodland and strongly recommend that you consider it.

WORK MARK

Eventually another day will come when an author will write a second book on the same subject as that of the first book the library has by him. If you use the initial of the first word in the title (other than an article —*a, an, the*) as a third line in the call number, each of these two books will have its own identification.

Another development that can occur as the library grows is acquiring a revised edition of a book already in the collection. In this case, use the date of the revised edition as the work mark of the call number to proclaim the difference between the two books.

BIOGRAPHY

One type of book whose call number will be created a bit differently is biography about an individual. All of these books will have the same classification number. For the book number, use the last name of the biographee rather than the author— either the first two or three letters of the name or the first letter plus the number from the Cutter-Sanborn table. This will then place all books about an individual together on the shelf. To bring an order among such books add a third line, the work mark, to the call number, using an *X* plus the author's last name, again either the first two or three letters or the first letter plus the number from the Cutter-Sanborn table.

Reference Books

If either of the first two classification systems is being used, place an *R* on the line above the call number on all reference books. The Union system uses an asterisk (*). The library committee should determine policy for these books: will they circulate freely as do all the other books in the collection, may they be checked out for use in church school classes only, or must they be used in the library? If it is decided that they must be used only in the library, it will not be necessary to prepare book cards and book pockets or straps for them.

Reference books should be shelved together and in order by call number at the beginning of the whole collection.

Catalog Cards

Although public, school, and other libraries type a various number of cards for each book for the public catalog, three cards are sufficient for the majority of books in the church library: an author card, a title card, and one subject card.

Definitions of terms used below to describe the form of these cards are: first indention—eight typewriter spaces from the left edge of the card; second indention—ten typewriter spaces from the left edge of the card; first line—two typewriter spaces from the top edge of the card.

Type all three cards for each book in this way:

Type the call number in the upper left corner, one space from the left edge, on the first and second lines (and on the third line for a work mark).

The name of the first author listed on the title page (for those books with more than one author) is typed at the first indention and on the second line. Give surname first, then given names in full if possible.

The title of the book as it appears on the *title page* begins at the second indention and on the third line. If it requires more than one line, all succeeding lines begin at first indention. Capitalize only the first word and proper names, follow the punctuation of the title page, and place a period at the end.

Space twice, then give the imprint which consists of place of publication, publisher, and date of publication. Many times this date is found on the verso (reverse side) of the title page and, if this is the case, it should be put in brackets. When the date is on the title page, the imprint is followed by a period; when the date is found some other place in the book and so is enclosed in brackets, no additional punctuation is necessary. If no date can be found, use *n.d.*

On the next line and at second indention, give the number of pages in the book followed by the letter *p* and a period. If the book is illustrated, space twice after the period and type *illus.*

If there is a bibliography, go to the next line, second indention, and type *Bibliography,* followed by a colon, the abbreviation *pp.,* and inclusive pages (for example, *Bibliography: pp. 96–99*).

AUTHOR CARD

The above information is basic to all books, with a few exceptions. If the author is an organization, association, corporation, institution, or society, the corporate name of the body responsible for the book is used as the author name. However, if a committee, department, or division of an institution or organization issued the book, the author line will show the name of the institution or organization first, followed by a period, then

```
UC72
K96      Kuntz, Kenneth A
            The congregation as church.  /Art work
         ... by Florence Dodson/  St. Louis, Beth-
         any Press /1971/
            176 p.   illus.
            Bibliography:  pp. 173-176.
```

FIG. 1. AUTHOR CARD

40

two spaces, the name of the committee, department, or division, and another period. If more than one line is needed for this information, the additional lines will be typed at the third indention—twelve typewriter spaces from the left edge of the card.

Anthologies and collections are gathered together by an editor or a compiler whose name is used, in that case, on the author line, followed by a comma and either *ed.* or *comp.*

For anoymous books whose author, compiler, corporate body, or editor cannot be determined from the title page or anywhere else, leave the author line blank. If this information is found at a later time, it can be added easily.

Some books have more than one author, in which case the first writer listed on the title page is considered the author. If three or fewer authors are involved, their names are given, in the order they are listed on the title page, after the title of the book. If more than three authors appear on the title page, use the first author's name followed by *and others* in this space after the title. If some of the authors other than the first one listed are important to your collection of books, one additional author card can be made for each such author, using his name, last name first, on the first line and at second indention.

Any words used on the catalog card that are not on the title page, such as a *by* between title and author, or an *and* used when there is more than one author, should be enclosed in brackets. Brackets can be made on a typewriter by using the slash (/) with the underline mark (L); for the top of the bracket the platen will need to be rolled down one space (Γ). The closing bracket looks like this: J . Notice that it is necessary to backspace once each time—for the opening bracket backspace for the bottom underline, for the closing bracket backspace for the top underline.

In addition to the basic information for all catalog cards, there will be other information for some books. If the book is a first edition *(1st ed.)*, a revised edition *(Rev. ed.)*, or a numbered edition *(2d ed., 5th ed.),* this information is given, in the form indicated, two spaces after the title and followed by two spaces before the imprint. However, if an illustrator is named on the title page, another entry is given before the imprint: *Illustrated by John Smith.* Very occasionally the contribution or the importance of the illustrator will justify an additional card for the card catalog giving the illustrator, last name first, on the first line and at second indention.

If the book is part of a series and the series is important, such as the Layman's Bible commentary or the Daily study Bible series (edited by William Barclay), this information is given in parentheses two spaces after the last item on the line that begins with the number of pages. If a second line is needed to complete this information, that line returns to the first indention. Capitalize only the first word and proper names, as in the two preceding examples.

TITLE AND SUBJECT CARDS

When these three cards are completed, one of them, as is, is the author card. On one of the other two cards, type the title, to its first punctuation, on the first line at the second indention—this is the title card. If the title is longer than one line, start a line

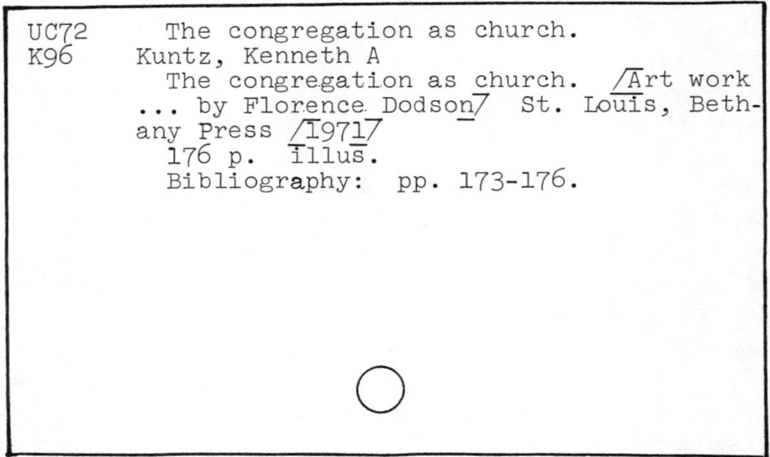

Fig. 2. Title Card

higher at the second indention and continue the title on the first line at third indention. In either case, capitalize the first word and proper names only and close with a period.

On the remaining card, at second indention and on the first line, type the subject of the book with all letters either capitalized or in red. A basic tool on subject headings is *Sears List of Subject Headings*. The tenth edition, edited by Barbara Westby, can be

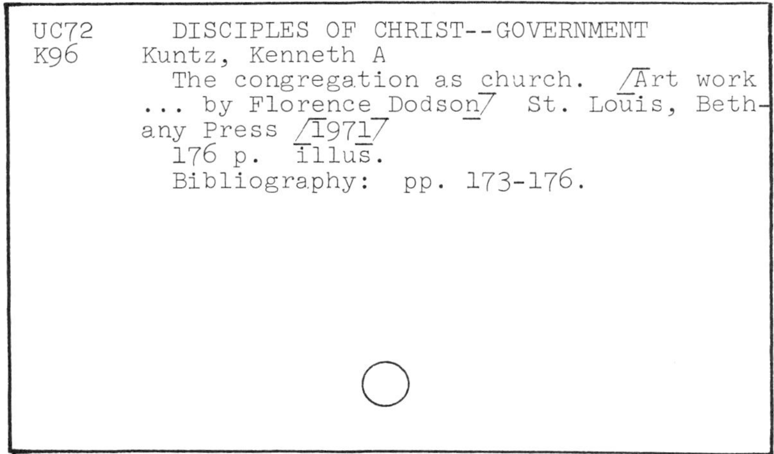

Fig. 3. Subject Card

purchased from H. W. Wilson Co., 950 University Avenue, New York, New York 10452, for $10.00. However, if you have chosen to use either the Numbered category system of classification or the Union system, such a tool would not really be necessary.

For some books it may be advisable or desirable to type more than one subject card. One such book for which a fourth card is necessary is a biography of an individual. On this card type the name of the biographee, in inverted form, on the first line at second indention.

Work Card/Author File

The work card, for workroom use as discussed in chapter 3, can be typed in the same way as the author card. In fact, if an error is made on one of the three cards being prepared for the public catalog, this card could become the work card. In practice, at Woodland we never discard any card on which the typing for the public catalog is not acceptable. We X through the spoiled side with pen or pencil and use the other either for a work card or for a consideration or order card.

For the work card, additional lines of information are given. One space from the left edge of the card on the next empty line,

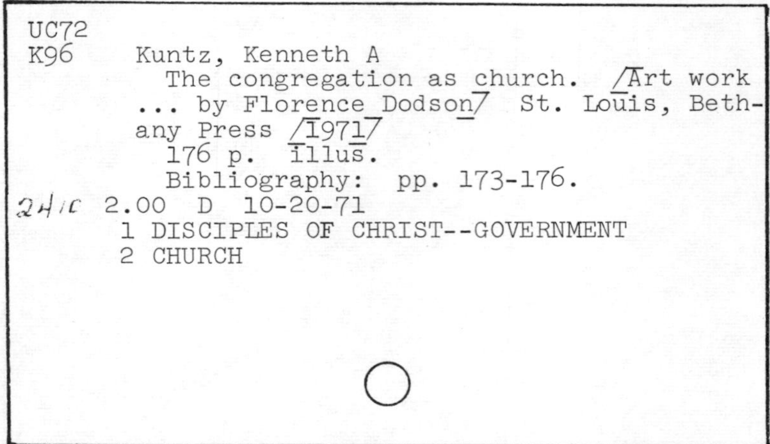

Fig. 4. Work Card/Author File

show the accession number (at Woodland we prefer to do this in red—either typed or with a ballpoint pen—to make it stand out), the cost, the source, and the date received. For a book purchased from the publisher, a *D* (for direct) can indicate the source and also be used on the order card when a book is ordered from the publisher. We find that spacing twice between each of these is sufficient; you may prefer to space more or to use the slash between each item.

On the next line (or more) show the subject heading(s) and any other headings used to indicate more than three cards in the card catalog, such as biographee, illustrator, series, etc. Such a note is called tracings, and the tracings may be shown on the back of the author card also.

These cards are filed alphabetically by author, and the file has several uses in addition to those given near the end of chapter 3. Once an author's full name has been located, a quick check of this file will supply it for any future books. If you have elected to use the Cutter-Sanborn table, the author's number on a card already in your file can be noted on the card for the new title. When more than one copy of a title is added to the library, accession numbers of the additional copies are noted on the card already in the file, as well as the cost, source, and date received. A new edition can also be indicated on the current work card by adding *rev. ed.* or *3d ed.* (or whatever) after the date received

44

plus the publication year of that edition. However, if the publisher or the number of pages or other information pertaining to the new edition varies greatly from the edition you have, it would be better to make a new work card for it.

You may discover other ways in which this file can be helpful. For instance, if the workroom is any distance from the card catalog, such a file will soon earn its keep in the number of trips it will save you between the two.

CONSIDERATION CARD/ORDER CARD/SHELF LIST CARD

The consideration file will also earn its keep many times over because each card, as it moves from the consideration file to the order file to the shelf list, will be at your beck and call while the title it represents is going through the preparation process.

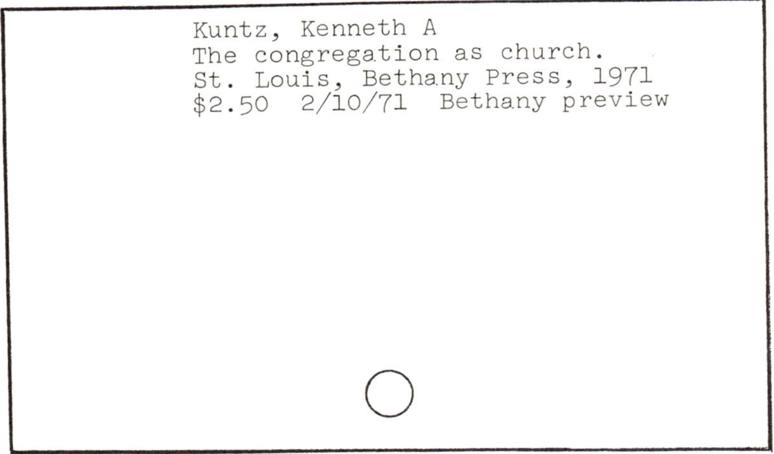

FIG. 5. CONSIDERATION CARD

Because this card will usually be prepared before you know all the necessary information about the book, a form slightly different from that on the other cards is more practical: type or write all lines at the third indention. Type or write the author's name on the first line, last name first; the title on the second line; the place, publisher, and date on the next empty line. Any of this information not known when the card is prepared for the consideration file can always be added at a later time. Make note

45

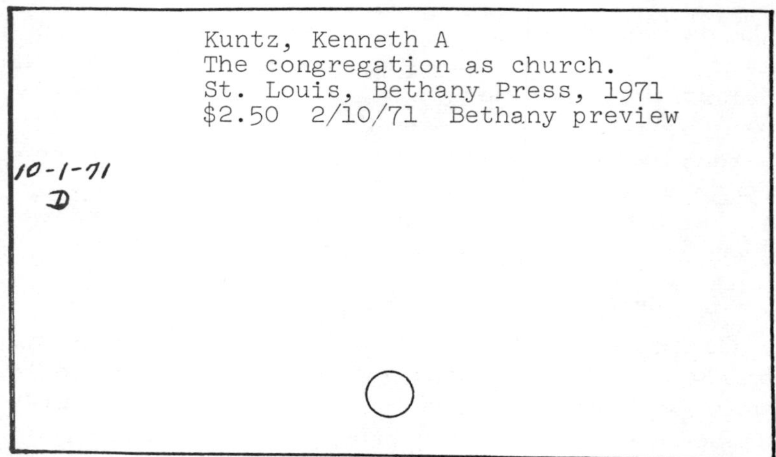

FIG. 6. ORDER CARD (WHEN BOOK IS ORDERED)

also of the price of the book and the date card is prepared for the consideration file.

When a book is to be ordered, pull its card from the consideration file. In the space on the lefthand edge of the card, perhaps a third of the way from the top, write the date of the order and from whom the book was ordered (using a *D* if it was the publisher). Depending on the size of the file, possibly

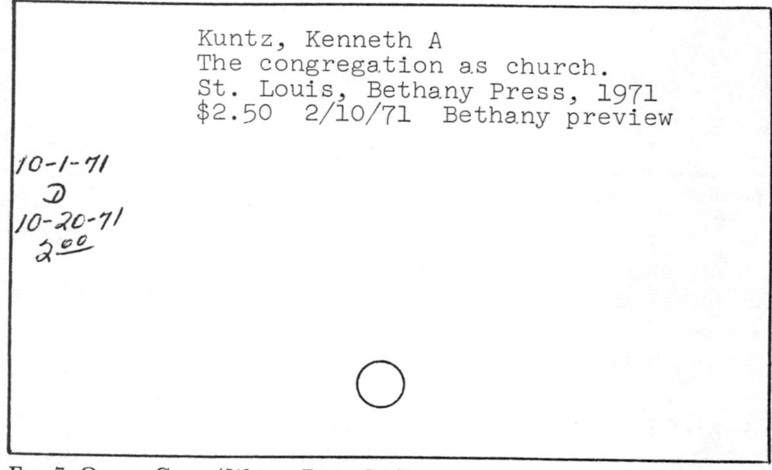

FIG. 7. ORDER CARD (WHEN BOOK IS RECEIVED)

46

the order in which the cards are arranged, and your preferences, this card, now an order card, can be returned to its original spot in the consideration file or to a separate order file, which might be immediately at the beginning or the end of the consideration file.

When ordered books begin to arrive, pull the order slip for each title and, below the order date and supplier, write or type the date each book is received and its cost. Keep the slip with the book until it has been accessioned and classified.

As books are processed, write on each slip, above the order date, the accession number of the book (at Woodland we use a red ballpoint pen or the red ink of the typewriter ribbon so that this number will stand out), and its call number on the top two or three lines on the lefthand side.

UC 72
K96 Kuntz, Kenneth A
The congregation as church. (A)
St. Louis, Bethany Press, 1971
2410 $2.50 2/10/71 Bethany preview
10-1-71 (A) [Art work ... by Florence Dodson]
D 176 p. illus.
10-20-71 Bibliography: pp. 173-176.
2.00

FIG. 8. SHELF LIST CARD

Now these cards are ready to become a part of the shelf list; each card will be filed into it by call number. In addition to the value and uses of the shelf list noted in the previous chapter, it will be helpful by calling to your attention the need for a work mark when a second title by the same author in the same area or when a later edition is added.

Book Card

The next step in preparing a book for circulation is to type one book card for each volume that will circulate. The accession number appears in the top right corner, first line; the call number is typed in the same order and location as on the three catalog cards; author's surname only at first indention on the second line; title at first indention on the fourth line. Beginning articles *(a, an, the)* may be omitted here, if you wish. Many times this will allow typing the title on one line. Succeeding lines are typed at second indention.

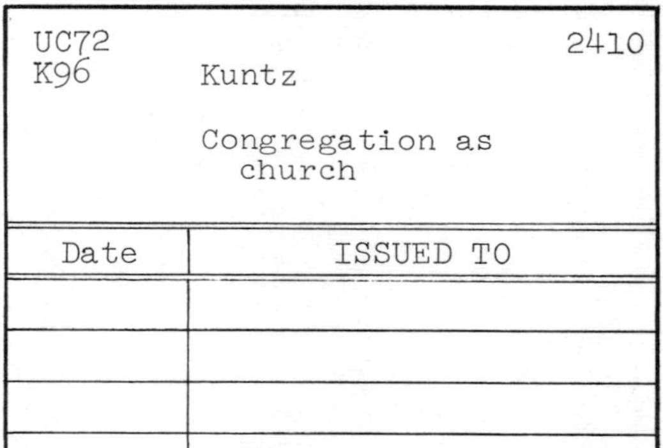

UC72 2410
K96 Kuntz

Congregation as
church

Date	ISSUED TO

Fig. 9. Book Card

If book pockets are used, type the call number and the accession number for each book in the same locations as on the book cards. If book straps are used, type the call number near the right side and a space or two from the top edge, then skip a line and type the accession number. Use the ownership stamp in the center and to the left of the typing.

Fig. 10. Book Strap

The book pocket or strap is pasted on the inside back cover. Date-due slips are not especially necessary, but if they are used they are pasted on the back flyleaf. Some books use endpapers with maps, drawings, or other information pertinent to the book. If the endpaper in back is different from the endpaper in front, it is advisable to choose the preceding two pages for the book pocket or strap and the date-due slip—provided, of course, that they are blank.

Facts about the author may be clipped from the dust jacket and pasted on the front flyleaf for the information of readers. If the book is a gift, the bookplate is pasted on the inside front cover, or an inscription may be written neatly there. Again, do not cover up special endpapers but rather use the following two pages.

Lettering

The last step is to letter the call number on the spine of the book. There are several ways to do this. One way is to paint with black india ink a strip across the spine of the book so that in every case the top of the strip is the same distance from the bottom of the book—two inches would be about right. When it is dry, use either pen and white ink or electric stylus and white transfer paper for the lettering. If the book is narrow, the lettering may go down the spine instead of across; if the book is very narrow, paint a square on the front cover close to the spine with black india ink, the same height as the strip on the back.

Another method is to type the call number on cloth gummed labels. The tops of the labels should all be the same height from the bottom of the book. Advantages of this method are that all the lettering will be the same regardless of who types the labels, and books will not have to wait to be lettered by someone with that talent. At Woodland we have found that covering the labels with Scotch Magic Transparent Tape that extends a short space beyond the label on both sides protects the typed call numbers and gives added assurance that the labels will not come off.

The lettering can, of course, be done directly on the book, at the same height, with a pen and black india ink on light covers and white ink on dark covers (or the stylus with black or white transfer paper). You will find that felt-tip pens work very nicely on most (although not all) paperbacks.

Regardless of what method is used, always spray the lettering with a transparent plastic coating to protect it from wear; in fact, the whole cover—front, back, spine—may be sprayed to brighten and protect it.

FILING CATALOG CARDS

When the preparation of books for circulation is completed, the catalog cards for them should be put in order and filed in the card catalog. A few simple rules need to be kept in mind so that the card catalog will be usable and so that more than one library helper can file into the catalog. Whether one or several people do the filing, have them leave the cards on top of the rods. Then periodically you can check the filing and at that time secure the cards with the rods.

50

The simple rules are:

- File alphabetically by words:
  > RELIGION
  > Religion and life.
  > RELIGION AND SCIENCE
  > Religion and the concept of democracy.
  > Religion's place in general education.
  > RELIGIOUS DRAMA

  A helpful rule to remember here is that nothing comes before something: RELIGION with nothing after it comes before RELIGION AND SCIENCE; that is religion with something after it.

- Disregard articles at the beginning of a title, but treat them as words if they occur elsewhere in the title.
- File names beginning with *M'*, *Mc*, or *Mac* as if they all were spelled *Mac*, and between *Mab* and *Mad*.
- File abbreviations as though they were spelled in full.
- File numerals as though they were spelled out.
- When the same word is used for person, place, subject, and title, arrange the cards in that order:
  > Church, Mary
  > CHURCH, N. DAK.
  > THE CHURCH
  > The church of our fathers.

Notice that the names for these types are in alphabetical order: person, place, subject, title. This will help you to remember the order in which these will be filed.

5

Preserving the Crop

CHECKING AND OPENING BOOKS

As books are received, and before any writing is done in them, check each page and page number to be certain that there are no blank pages and each signature is accounted for in proper order but not duplicated. If errors are found, write to the publisher or the supplier for a new copy in exchange for the bad one. Occasionally pages are not cut and this is the time to do it, carefully, with a sharp penknife or letter opener.

Another time-consuming operation but a very worthwhile one is to open new books properly. This is one of those processes the librarian can assign to a library helper or a member of the library committee. Holding the book upright with its spine on a table or other firm surface, press down each cover, close to the spine, gently but firmly. Now go through the entire book this way, doing a few pages at a time and alternating sides. This process will lengthen the life of each new book.

BOOK SUPPORTS

When the final steps of preparation are completed, each book can be put in its place on the proper shelf. Before too many books are on shelves, the need for bookends or book supports will become very obvious. Library supply houses carry two sizes of bookends in metal and in plastic in several colors. Most libraries will need very few of the larger size, but some uses for these would be children's books, large books, sets, and reference books. Of the regular size, the plastic ones in several colors could be used to give added color to otherwise drab surroundings.

If money is too scarce for book supports, especially in the early days of the library, they can be made from bricks covered with heavy paper or cloth or from old license plates. License plates are bent, edges are smoothed, and they are painted bright colors. However, they, even more than metal bookends, can damage books being returned to the shelves, so do be careful.

FILLING SHELVES TWO-THIRDS

Books are shelved from left to right by call number, and shelves should never be filled more than two-thirds. *Never* may be too strong a word because there will be times, as new titles are added, that shelves will get too full. But never, never force one more book on the too-full shelf—coming and going will be destructive to it and the books around it. Crowded shelves may be corrected by adding more shelving or by weeding.

WEEDING

Weeding is that process by which out-of-date books are sought out and removed from the collection. Among out-of-date books are those whose scientific or statistical information is no longer correct, and those depicting outmoded situations and methods in missions work. A rule of thumb that may be helpful is to question whether the material covered is accurate, authoritative, factual, reliable, up-to-date. If one or more of these characteristics is lacking in a book, it needs to be considered for discarding.

The decision to discard may be a difficult one. Some well-meaning people have suggested that the results of one library's weeding can be donated to another, presumably poorer, library. My feeling, however, is that if a book is not good enough for one library it is not good enough for any other library. Therefore, unless a book has potential or actual historical value, discarding means throwing away—to recycling or to a junk pile. Well, perhaps another exception can be made to so drastic an action: if possible, discarded books could be made available to people learning or relearning to read who have not the means to buy books; in this case, content would be far down on the scale of priorities.

A third exception could be to sell or trade these books with a secondhand bookdealer if one is close by. Selling would provide additional funds; trading would involve establishing a credit balance with the dealer against which purchases could be made whenever he has books your library has been wanting.

OVERSIZE BOOKS

Oversize books need special handling in shelving. With adjustable shelves, it is possible to shelve them upright in their rightful places; however, if there is only one oversize book on a shelf, but there are several such shelves in a section, too much space may be lost. There are at least two alternatives in such a situation. The book may be shelved in its proper place but with its spine on the shelf. Or one shelf may be used for all oversize books. If shelving is not adjustable, these books may be laid flat. When this second method is chosen, the cards in the catalog and in the workroom should carry the notation *oversize* above the call number.

OTHER PRECAUTIONS

The starch and glue used in bookmaking are especially attractive to several kinds of undesirable bugs, so some precaution should be taken to discourage this kind of patron. If the church uses the services of an exterminator, request that the library be included.

DUSTING

An attractive library is one that, among other things, is dusted regularly, and this applies to both shelves and books. Because book covers absorb oil, do not use oily dustcloths or sprays with an oil base. A solution of one part vinegar and four parts warm water is easily prepared and may be used occasionally. Use cheesecloth dipped in the solution and then squeezed until it is only damp. After wiping the book covers lightly, allow them to dry and then spray them again with the plastic spray before returning them to the shelves. While they are drying, the shelves may be wiped with a cloth dampened in the vinegar-water solution.

REPAIRING

Anytime the books are dusted as well as when they return from circulating are good times to watch for those that may be in need of repair. Easy repairs include loose book pockets or straps and date-due slips that just need to be repasted, and torn pages that can be mended with Scotch Brand Magic Mending Tape—*never* Scotch Tape.

Repairs a little more difficult or time-consuming include loose pages, which can be secured by putting a very thin line of liquid plastic adhesive (from a bottle with a thin pouring spout) on the spine-edge of the page and carefully inserting it as close as possible to the spine. The pages on either side may be protected by strips of waxed paper positioned near the spine. Another repair in this category is loose spines, which may also be secured with the liquid plastic adhesive, or with Mystic Cloth Tape. This is the trade name for Gaylord's product. The other supply companies have a similar tape bearing their trade names. If tape is used, the spine will need to be relettered with the author, title, and call number.

BOOKBINDING

For the more difficult repairs, each library committee must decide the extent to which it will commit its funds. Book repair kits, which usually include an instruction manual, can be purchased from library supply companies. A committee member or library helper with an aptitude for this kind of work might enjoy doing the repairs or rebinding. Otherwise, it might be well to inquire of the public library where its binding is done and make arrangements to send books to that bindery. This can be quite expensive and the library committee must decide the wisdom of using its money this way. Books still in print and of lasting value could be replaced; however, at today's prices, binding might actually be cheaper.

If or when books are sent to a bindery, use the book cards to show the date the books are sent and the bindery, and file them together at the end of the charged-out file. When the books are returned, continue using the book cards, type new book pockets or straps and paste them in, letter the books and spray them, and they are ready to be shelved.

Another service project that the library could encourage if funds are available is to have the church paper and bulletin bound as permanent additions to the library. If the church has a historian, this person could be responsible for collecting the weekly publications, keeping them in proper order, and submitting them to the library for binding annually. If there is no church historian, one of the library workers can be responsible for this. And while this person is collecting one set of these publications, it is just as easy to collect a second set which can be sent to the denominational historical society as another contribution to the historical picture of that denomination.

In the organizational setup of some churches, the secretary of the governing body changes annually or perhaps every two years, and frequently in this changing process the minutes of previous years get misplaced or lost. The library can suggest that these very valuable records also be bound at regular intervals, at the expense of the governing body of course, whether or not they are placed in the library after they are bound.

6

Cultivating the Growth

Before books actually begin to circulate, the librarian and the library committee need to consider policies, procedures, and rules. When these have been established, they must be posted and explained to borrowers. It is well, from time to time, to remind users of some of the regulations by publishing them in the church paper.

HOURS

One of the first items to consider is the hours the library will be open with the librarian or an assistant on duty. Many churches have found that most patrons use the library on Sunday mornings. For this reason the library committee should schedule assistants at least one half hour before church school and after the morning service and for any time between the two. The committee should consider the advisability of having assistants available before and after scheduled meetings during the week also. Although various groups meeting during the week may not be aware of the ways in which the library resources could assist them, this would be an ideal way and time for the librarian or assistant on duty to bring those resources suitable to each group to its attention.

LOAN PERIOD

Another item to be considered is the length of time books may be checked out and whether books may be renewed. The usual length of time is two weeks, although the committee should consider the pros and cons of a three-week period. Renewals might be permitted if no one else has requested the book, and two renewals should be the limit.

Because the majority of books will be checked out on Sundays, due dates should be Sundays. Immediately at the close of library hours each Sunday, the date-due stamp should be changed to the following Sunday, which means that books charged out during the week may be kept a bit longer than the usual loan period.

FINES

This leads to a third item: fines. Presently, for church libraries, ten cents a week seems to be the amount if it is decided to charge fines. And if it is decided to charge fines, it is well to stress that these are not penalties; rather, they are contributions to the finances of the library.

Some library committees, rather than imposing a fine, prefer to keep a piggy-bank type of box where books are returned so that patrons who wish to may make a contribution when they are late returning books.

A librarian friend tells of the elderly gentleman who, on several occasions, was charged a fine for returning books late. Then came the morning when he returned some books and triumphantly demanded his money—he had returned the books before they were due, so the library owed him a fine.

OVERDUE NOTICES

Whether or not fines are used, there should be a system for sending overdue notices within a reasonable time after a book becomes due. This could be a postcard telling the patron that the records show such-and-such a book, checked out by him, was due last Sunday, and asking him to please return it next Sunday. Or the library committee may decide that its policy will be to telephone individuals or see them in person. In this case, committee members or library assistants responsible for making these contacts must be diligent about the task. A shut-in who can do such telephoning or card-sending could be included as a member of the library committee.

REPLACING BOOKS

A fifth item for consideration is the very occasional lost or damaged book. The committee should determine a policy for such an occasion long before it ever happens. Shall the person responsible for the loss or damage be charged full value of the book at the time it was purchased or at the present time when the price may be higher? If the book is outdated or out of print, should an effort be made to locate another copy, or would it be better to purchase an updated book in the same area? The answer depends, in part, on whether the library has relatively easy access to used-book shops; in part, on the book that was lost or damaged—was it one that would soon be considered for weeding or was it a new book recently purchased?

The procedure for checking books out and in will vary from library to library, but the most common way is for patrons to sign the book card in each book they wish to take out. The librarian on duty will stamp the date due in the book and on the book card. A helpful hint, particularly at peak times, is to remember to stamp the book first because the patron will take it away, and because there are several patrons waiting. The book cards can be stamped later when the rush is over.

Some libraries file the book cards by the call number, some use the accession number, others file alphabetically by author, and a few may file alphabetically by title. Whichever method is used, all book cards with the same due date are filed together, with a divider to separate the due dates. When books are returned, the cards are found and inserted in the proper book pocket or strap, and the book is then ready to be replaced on the shelf. A safety device to be sure the right card gets in the right book is to check the accession number on the card with the one in the book because only one book will have each accession number.

It will be helpful to patrons, especially if they may check out books at times when no one is on duty, to have posters or other guides giving instructions on how to check out books and other circulation information at the place where this is done. From time to time, as a part of the promotion of the library, such information could be carried in the weekly news bulletin also.

When the last line of a book card has been used, a new card can be made and clipped to the filled card until the book is returned. Unless you have a great amount of storage space in which to file these filled cards, it is better to discard them.

Woodland's library, as stated in earlier chapters, is in a busy hall, and it seldom has had a library committee. Because of its location, it is always open. The librarian is usually available before and after services on Sunday morning to give assistance to any users needing help. We do not have a loan period, so we have no fines and only occasionally do we send overdue notices.

Our system for checking books out and in has been determined, of course, by our location. Anyone may, at any time the church is open, check out a book by signing his name on the book card and noting the date. The card is left in a recipe file box on top of our low bookcases. Each Sunday it is part of my schedule to take the cards from the box, check the dates written (or rather not written) on the cards, arrange them alphabetically by author, and interfile them with the cards from books taken out earlier in the year. These are kept in a small box that goes back and forth with me. This method has been devised because it allows me to know when books are returned and prevents a borrower from putting the wrong card in a returned book.

For returned books we have a medium-sized cardboard box appropriately marked and beside the recipe box so that borrowers may return books anytime the church is open. Each Sunday my schedule includes removing the books from the box, finding and inserting the correct book cards, and reshelving the books. This is not an ideal system: cards have been left in the recipe box without signatures, or no card has been left—the borrower has taken it with the book.

Records

With the official opening of the library, and even before, one of the more important responsibilities of the librarian is to keep records. Regardless of the source of finances for the library, an accurate record of receipts and expenditures should be maintained so that periodic reports can be made to the library committee and to the governing body of the church, especially when it is from this group that budget money comes.

The extent to which circulation records are kept will vary from library to library. Some will keep only a record of the number of books circulated each week. Others may choose to keep their records in more detail by noting the numbers circulated in each category. This will show the more popular areas as well as the areas that may need developing, and it will also show areas that may need more promoting.

Promotion

Speaking of promoting brings us to another of the major areas of responsibility for the librarian and the library committee. Even though the library is neat, attractive, well arranged, and has a good collection of books, it will be used far from capacity without constant promotion. The universal plea of church librarians is, How can we get people to read the good books in the library? The answer, of course, is to tell potential patrons about those good books as often and in as many ways as possible. The only limitation to a capable, concerned, enthusiastic librarian coping with promotion is imagination.

Ways to promote are the use of reading clubs, bulletin boards, posters, book jackets, announcements in the church paper and a regular column telling about books—especially new ones, book displays, quoteboards, skits at supper meetings, reading lists, book tables at special meetings, and bookmarks.

Times to promote, besides constantly, include special seasons and holidays and during National Library Week in April or, for Disciples of Christ, Christian Literature Week in the fall. Birthdays, anniversaries, homecoming, areas of study, and social concerns also offer opportunities for promotion.

In addition to book jackets, use colors, flowers, pipe cleaner figures, materials of various weights and textures, finger painting, and artistic efforts of local people—perhaps a member of the library committee.

In addition to the display area in or near the library, have displays in as many classrooms and meeting areas as possible, and plan the displays with the age level and interest of those using the classrooms or meeting areas in mind. Change displays at least monthly.

Be aware of the church calendar, both for the local congregation and for the church year, and plan library activities and displays to coordinate with the various programs. When plans are being made for a leadership training course, be sure the library has resources for the course and publicize them. If a homecoming is being planned, make displays using bound volumes of the church's weekly bulletins and pictures of individuals and groups from earlier years. Make youth groups aware of books in the library that will help them plan meetings and answer some of the weighty problems they have. Parents will appreciate knowing about books in the library that will help them understand teenagers. Meet with lay leaders of various areas of concern in the church's program and acquaint each with the resources pertaining to his area of responsibility.

Even reference work is a kind of promotion. A person comes asking how and where to find information on a particular subject. The librarian's task is to show the questioner what is available on that subject, and in doing so may make that person aware for the first time of the extent of the library's resources. Once the patron knows what is available on the subject, the librarian should let him make his own choice from that material.

Another kind of promotion occurs when as many persons as possible are involved on the library committee or as library workers. Helpers can range from fifth or sixth graders to retired persons. Each one will soon become a library promoter among his peers as well as other persons and groups with which he is associated.

Two very helpful publications to know about for promotion ideas are *Promoting Your Church Library*[1] and *Media: Library Services Journal,* the latter recommended in chapter 3 as a source under book selection.

1. Marian S. Johnson, *Promoting Your Church Library* (Minneapolis: Augsburg Publishing House, 1968).

7

Sights, Sounds, and Seasoning

Up to this point the discussion has been only about books, with a hint now and then about other media. A real service library will also include other kinds of material: periodicals, pamphlets, pictures, films, filmstrips, slides, records, and cassettes.

PERIODICALS

Each denomination publishes perhaps a half-dozen magazines for its membership, and each library should consider subscribing to as many of these as its budget will allow. In addition to the periodicals from your publishing house, there are several very good ones from interdenominational and nondenominational sources that should find a place in every library because of their contributions to Christian knowledge and growth.

Library supply companies carry magazine racks, some of which have storage space for back issues in addition to the display area for current issues. Also available in various sizes are storage boxes for back issues. An alternative, again depending on budget, is binding back issues, in which case each bound volume will be accessioned as a book and classified as a reference book, with a single card in the card catalog for each title. Of course, not all periodicals will have permanent value; those that don't can be discarded eventually after each issue is checked carefully for single articles that may be worth clipping for an information file.

Pamphlets are a source of information on many subjects and they, like periodicals, often begin developing a new area or idea before books appear. But there is the usual question of how to handle them. Some libraries (Woodland is one of these) treat them the same as books, shelving them in their proper relation to the rest of the library collection. Most libraries, however, prefer to put them in folders and file them by subject in a file cabinet. If pamphlets are treated as books, each one will have its cards in the card catalog. If pamphlets are filed by subject, there should be one card in the card catalog for each subject with a notation that material on this subject will be found in the information file (sometimes called a vertical file).

Another way of handling pamphlets is discussed in *The Pamphlet Library* by Dale Eugene Shaffer and dated 1972. A copy can be ordered from Dale E. Shaffer, Library Consultant, 437 Jennings Avenue, Salem, Ohio 44460.

INFORMATION FILE

Additional information on the various subjects covered by pamphlets, as well as other subjects, will often be found in such sources as newspapers, magazines, and church papers. This information can be clipped and added to the proper folder. All clipped material should have noted on it the source from which it came and the date. It is extremely important that such an information file be weeded at regular intervals because much of this kind of information becomes quickly outdated, and some of it will be replaced by books. Stated even more strongly, unless such an information file is weeded periodically it would be better not to start one.

PICTURES

Most denominational publishing houses include in their curriculum material sets of pictures relating to the subject matter of each unit, especially for the younger grades. The church library would be an excellent place in which to put a complete set of these pictures, not only for the teachers, but also for others who may wish to borrow them for short periods of time. Other suitable pictures may be added to these from various sources, including magazines.

Very good reproductions of famous pictures and religious masterpieces are now available already framed and relatively inexpensively priced. As money is available, these could be added one or two at a time. It would be well to keep a separate accession book for pictures, or a separate section at the end of the book accession record, but they need not be classified. Instead, prepare one card for the catalog, type *Picture* in the space for the call number, and file these cards alphabetically by artist and separately from all the other cards by placing them either at the very beginning of the card catalog or at the very end. Another method that may be even more helpful to library users would be to use colored catalog cards, type the same three cards as for books, and file them into the card catalog in the same way. On the back of the picture use the ownership stamp, paste a book pocket or strap, and insert a regular book card with the artist's name and the title of the picture. Borrowers should be permitted to keep these pictures for a longer period of time, perhaps a month or six weeks.

Dale E. Shaffer has prepared *The Library Picture File (A Complete System of How to Process and Organize)*, published in 1970. A copy can be secured by sending fifty cents to Dale E. Shaffer, Library Consultant, 437 Jennings Avenue, Salem, Ohio 44460. Although it is written primarily for elementary, secondary, and college libraries, most of the information can be adapted for the church library. It includes "Sources of Pictures, Charts, Study Units, and Maps."

MAPS

Maps are another kind of resource material that a church library can provide. The majority of these probably would be of the Holy Land, Paul's journeys, and the countries in which your denomination does mission work. If there are only a few maps, these could be placed in one folder in the information file, provided they are the kind that can be folded. If they are the larger rolled maps, perhaps someone in the congregation who makes furniture for a hobby could make a suitable case in which to store them.

A library that really becomes the hub of its congregation's activities will be the first place people will come for many things besides books. It may become the guardian of worship equipment, curios representative of mission fields supported by the denomination, world globes, and any number of other nonbook items. Storage space may become a problem, but who knows how many of the people who come for these things will turn into avid readers.

AUDIO-VISUALS

More and more church libraries are assuming responsibility for audio-visuals: films, filmstrips, slides, records, and cassettes. Careful consideration must be given to these materials in relation to the budget. Many smaller libraries may need to delay for some time a venture into audio-visuals.

A further consideration by all libraries will be the extent to which the equipment for using audio-visuals can be purchased, and even whether it should be purchased from the library budget. Either the library budget will need to be increased considerably to take care of purchasing the expensive equipment, or this should be an additional item in the church's budget. It would be most exceptional for all the pieces of equipment to be purchased at one time; therefore, a modest sum could be included each year as a carry-over item for equipment and each piece purchased when enough money had accumulated. Either the library committee or a special committee for the purpose will need to prepare a list of equipment in order of preferred purchase. This committee should remember to include an item for upkeep and repair of all equipment.

FILMS

Films usually are too expensive to purchase, especially if they are for only one or two showings; it is much better to rent them. If the library will be taking the responsibility for renting films for use by various classes or groups, there must be a clear understanding from the very beginning about who will be charged for the rental.

Filmstrips are not expensive to purchase, especially if the subject matter will be pertinent for several years. Probably those dealing with leadership and teacher training and with subjects of special concern and interest to the youth will make up the largest portion of filmstrips. Most denominations have an agency responsible for audio-visuals that can be consulted about equipment and can supply many, if not all, of the filmstrips and other media your library will be interested in purchasing or renting. Library supply houses carry several kinds of storage containers for filmstrips, and you can choose the kind that will be best for the collection in your library.

Again it would be advisable to use an accession record separate from that for books and for pictures. Filmstrips can be classified by the same system used for books, with the addition of *Filmstrip* or *FS* on the line above the call number. Some libraries also use catalog cards of another color so that someone looking for a filmstrip need not thumb through all the cards or so that someone who does not want a filmstrip and may overlook the notation at the beginning of the call number can be alerted by the color.

The majority of filmstrips have a user's guide from which the narration can be read, and many of them have, in addition, a record. These should show the same accession number as the filmstrip, and they should be noted on the catalog card. The reading script could be equipped with a book packet or strap and a book card, which would serve for the two or three pieces of each filmstrip.

There are a number of sets of filmstrips having from two to a dozen strips. The more there are in a set, the more expensive the set is. You might contact other churches in your neighborhood or in your denomination with the suggestion that all go together to purchase those sets that all the participating churches could use.

A suggested policy of the library for audio-visuals and equipment would be that all such material must be reserved a week before it is to be used. However, the length of time is arbitrary; for some libraries, twenty-four hours may be sufficient notice. The second part of the policy would be that all audio-visuals and equipment must be returned promptly after they are used.

All that has been said about filmstrips applies as well to slides, with the additional caution to be sure that the last slide of a set is removed from the projector.

TAPES AND CASSETTES

Tapes and cassettes may not be in too many church library collections yet, but the latter, especially, are rapidly being produced with material of value for all phases of church life and program. Handling both tapes and cassettes should be done in the same way as filmstrips.

Library supply catalogs show various file cabinets constructed especially for storage of slides, tapes, and cassettes, but these may be too expensive, particularly for libraries with low budgets. If so, perhaps a drawer in the file cabinet or one in the desk or empty boxes once containing catalog or book cards can be adapted as storage containers.

Except for pamphlets and four or five periodical titles that have been given to us bound by volumes, Woodland's library has no responsibility for the other media at present.

A COOPERATIVE COMMUNITY PROJECT

In a community with several churches of the same denomination, each church of that denomination prepared an inventory list of its films, filmstrips, slides, and equipment, and these lists were gathered together in one church. A compilation of all audio-visuals in the area was made from them and sent to all participating churches. In this way each church knows what is available and where. Borrowing and lending is carried on by the two churches involved. Only one church purchases a given item, thus allowing each audio-visual budget to go much farther than it had in the past by eliminating duplicate purchasing. All purchasing of new material is cleared through the church in which the inventory lists are located; the central location is notified when new purchases are received and disperses this information to participating churches.

It is hoped that as this project is refined other denominations in the community will be encouraged to send their inventory lists and the project will become an ecumenical one among all the churches in that community.

8

Breaking Fresh Ground

Groups

From time to time we have suggested various groups and interests that the librarian should remember when books and other materials are selected. Curriculum aids for all age levels; mission study aids; material on the various program areas of the church, such as stewardship, evangelism, social concerns, worship, and personal enrichment; and materials for families are among those that historically have been a responsibility of the library committee.

Individuals

More recently there has been a growing concern for special individuals in the community and in the church. Special individuals include shut-ins, the hospitalized, the physically handicapped, the mentally retarded, nonreaders and poor readers, unmarried persons, widows, homosexuals, and elderly persons. Material is appearing about and for some of these for the first time. Shut-in, hospitalized, and physically handicapped individuals may welcome books brought to them from the church library and, in some cases, persons to read to them. Some church libraries with sufficient personnel are providing assistance to nonreaders and poor readers as a supplement to the school system. Due to shorter work weeks and earlier retirement, more books have been appearing on hobbies and on preparing for retirement years. For some time there have been books *about* the mentally retarded, but just recently books and church school study courses have been appearing *for* these people. The library committee must determine its responsibility to provide material for all these special individuals, as well as about them, so that responsible church members can understand the more complex individuals in some of these categories and learn how to work with them.

Things to Know About

The last several years have been marked by more rapid changes, new concerns, and new movements than at any time previously. Many long-lived periodicals have been forced to retire from publication because of the high cost of paper, postage, and personnel. At the same time many new journals, magazines, and news sheets have come to life, their purpose being to help us cope with all the changes, with our concerns, with the action and movement around us and in which we may be involved. A few of these newer publications have come to my attention and it occurred to me that *knowing* about them could help a church library be of greater service to its questing, confused, searching patrons: hence appendix A. Whether or not a church library chooses to subscribe to or purchase one or more of these will be a decision for its library committee to make, and will depend to some degree on the wise use of financial resources.

Before any decision is made, however, it would be time well spent to visit your public library to see which of the titles in appendix A are already being received there and to check on the possibility of the public library's subscribing to others on the list. This kind of information can be noted right in this book beside the titles for quick reference about the availability of material in any given area about which a patron might inquire.

This list of "things to know about" contains only a few of those now available, but many of these publications list or make reference to additional sources of information in their areas. Not all of the titles are new; some older ones have been included because they are worth knowing about. The entries in appendix A are listed alphabetically by title and include publisher, address, price, and, where necessary and/or known, a brief comment.

Please note: The titles listed in appendix A are *not* given because a church library should consider subscribing to them. The primary purpose of the list is precisely what the heading of this section says: things to *know* about. Be aware of them, that they exist, that the kinds of information and help they offer may just point the way to answers a patron needs.

70

Do enjoy being the church librarian! The twinkle in your eye and the spring in your step plus the goodies in the library will make you a most valuable minister to your church, and the ministry of that library will influence generations far beyond your knowledge.

APPENDIX A

Sources to Know About

Arts and activities. 8150 North Central Park Avenue, Skokie, IL 60076. $7.00 per year. "The teacher's arts and crafts guide." Primarily for public school teachers, but the excellent ideas and helpful ads can benefit church school teachers also.

Black Books Bulletin. Institute of Positive Education. 7850 South Ellis Avenue, Chicago, IL 60619. $6.00 per year. ". . . presents current, annotated listings of the newest writings by and about Black People. . . . Black Publishing Houses . . . present news and announcements about their work and plans."

Chorister's Guild Letters. Chorister's Guild. 440 Northlake Center, Dallas, TX 75238. $6.00 per year for regular membership. The guild develops "Christian character through children's choirs."

Church and State. Americans United for Separation of Church and State. 8120 Fenton Street, Silver Spring, MD 20910. $5.00 per year. Dedicated to preserving the constitutional principle of church-state separation.

engage/Social Action. Board of Church and Society of the United Methodist Church and Council for Christian Social Action of the United Church of Christ. 100 Maryland Avenue, N.E., Washington, DC 20002. One year, $5.00; two years, $9.00; three years, $12.00. Deals with Christian social action, interpreting social issues, the influence of the church in the life of this society.

Fellowship in Prayer. 200 East 36th Street, Room 10-E, New York, NY 10016. $3.00 per year. Promotes the practice of prayer among all religious faiths whose fundamental belief is in God, regardless of race, creed, or color, and whose tenets include the universal attributes of truth, honesty, justice, and mercy.

Fish International Newsletter. Jarrow Press. 18 Main Street, Lennox, MA 01240. $3.00 per year. An ecumenical lay ministry, "originating in England and now worldwide, Fish is a movement of people helping people. Largely though not exclusively organized in Christian churches, Fish came into being for two reasons—to meet the need of an organization ready to offer help, and to provide a way of fulfilling the Lord's commandment to love our neighbor. The members of Fish commit themselves to a particular amount of time each week to be 'on call' to those who ask for help."

The Humanist. 923 Kensington Avenue, Buffalo, NY 14215. One year, $6.00; two years, $10.00; three years, $13.50. "A journal of humanist and ethical concern" that "attempts to serve as a bridge between theoretical philosophical discussions and the practical applications of humanism to ethical and social problems."

i.e. Ecumenical Institute. 3444 West Congress Parkway, Chicago, IL 60624. No subscription, but contribution of $5.00 per year. The institute is a spiritual movement developed to lead congregations in the task of religious and social renewal.

IDOC-North America. International Documentation on the Contemporary Church. 235 East 49th Street, New York, NY 10017. Monthly, $25.00 per year. Deals with vital social issues affecting interfaith relations, human and community development, ecology, the plight of oppressed peoples in all areas of the world, and the struggle to form values appropriate to the changing conditions of our world.

IFCO News. The Interreligious Foundation for Community Organization, Inc. 475 Riverside Drive, Room 560, New York, NY 10027. No subscription fee, but contributions urgently needed. IFCO is an ecumenical agency established to support self-help projects of minority communities. Nine national religious agencies and one civic foundation promote, fund, and coordinate nationwide community organization and development efforts. IFCO is one of the few nationwide groups working at the task of community organization.

Liberation. 339 Lafayette Street, New York, NY 10012. One year, $7.00; two years, $13.00. A radical monthly magazine publishing articles by people involved in the struggle to achieve a more fully human society based on the principles of libertarian socialism.

Mass Media Ministries Bi-weekly Newsletter. Mass Media Associates, Inc. 2116 North Charles Street, Baltimore, MD 21218 (also 1720 Chouteau Avenue, St. Louis, MO 63103). $10.00 per year. A service devoted to a responsible encounter between the church and the arts. Includes up-to-date information about films and filmstrips, and calls attention to significant plays, recordings, books, and upcoming television programs.

Mid-Stream. Council on Christian Unity. 222 South Downey, Indianapolis, IN 46207. $5.00 per year. Brings to the attention of members and friends significant materials on ecumenical issues.

Money. Time-Life Building, 541 North Fairbanks Court, Chicago, IL 60611. $15.00 per year. A monthly magazine about money management, personal and family.

Newsletter. Institute for Urban Ministries. 222 E. 5th Street, Tulsa, OK 74103. $3.00 per year. Produced to facilitate communications among seminarians. Although beamed to seminarians, it is an excellent way to "eavesdrop" on many subjects pertinent to today.

Praying Hands. 28 Church Street, Room 14, Winchester, MA 01890. Free on request. A medium for the interchange of ideas, experiences, and plans among groups and organizations contemplating religious programs; for providing stimulating material; for serving men and women in the professions.

Renewal. 235 East 49th Street, New York, NY 10017. $4.00 per year. An independent journal of opinion, reporting, and interpretation of matters of concern to the religious community. Its purpose is to stimulate a critical review of the church's role in renewing the physical, moral, and spiritual aspects of our secular society.

Reporter, for Conscience' Sake. National Interreligious Service Board for Conscientious Objectors. 550 Washington Bldg., 15th and New York Avenue, N.W., Washington, DC 20005. One year, $2.50; two years, $4.00; three years, $6.00.

Review of Books and Religion. P.O. Box 2, Belmont, VT 05730. $3.50 per year. A medium through which readers can keep up with the new books conveying ideas, trends, and movements in contemporary religion.

Simulation Sharing Service. P.O. Box 1176, Richmond, VA 23209. $5.00 per year. An ecumenical communication link, primarily for religious educators, to enable the sharing of discoveries in gaming and to promote the use of simulation/gaming in the church's ministry. A very good resource for locating other publishers and users of simulation, and for promoting those you know about to others.

Spiritual Frontiers. Spiritual Frontiers Fellowship, Inc. 800 Custer Avenue, Suite 1, Evanston, IL 60202. $5.00 per year. Goals of the fellowship: " ' to sponsor, explore and interpret the growing interest in psychic phenomena and mystical experience within the church, wherever these experiences relate to effective prayer, spiritual healing and personal survival'; to develop 'spiritual growth in the individual and [encourage] new dimensions of spiritual experience within the church.' It is Christian in origin and emphasis, interdenominational in scope, and inter-faith in pursuit of its ultimate goal."

Tempo. Department of Information, National Council of Churches. 475 Riverside Drive, New York, NY 10027. $2.00 per year. "An ecumenical publication of the National Council of Churches."

Worldview. Council on Religion and International Affairs. 170 East 64th Street, New York, NY 10021. One year, $10.00; two years, $18.00; three years, $25.00. Grapples with the policy *and* the premise, the is *and* the ought of public issues, trying to define the vital links between American interests and moral imperatives. Includes a correspondence column adequate to the response that thoughtful and controversial articles provoke; sound judgments on a wide range of books; and comments, when appropriate, on the impact of other media, including the movies.

APPENDIX B

Library Supply and Equipment Companies

American Instructional Materials, Inc., Box 22748, Texas Woman's University Station, Denton, TX 76204.

Bro-Dart, Inc. Eastern Division: 1609 Memorial Avenue, Williamsport, PA 17701 *or* 56 Earl Street, Newark, NJ 07114; Western Division: 15255 E. Don Julian Road, City of Industry, CA 91746.

Demco Educational Corp., P.O. Box 1488, Madison, WI 53701.

Fordham Equipment Company, 2377–79 Hoffman Street, Bronx, NY 10458.

Gaylord Bros., Inc., P.O. Box 61, Syracuse, NY 13201 *or* P.O. Box 710, Stockton, CA 95201.

The Highsmith Co., Inc., P.O. Box 25, Fort Atkinson, WI 53538.

Josten's American Library Line (supplies), 4070 Shirley Drive S.W., Atlanta, GA 30336.

Josten's Library Services Division, 900 East 80th Street, Minneapolis, MN 55420.

The following companies supply furniture and metal stacks primarily:

Art Metal Construction Co., Jamestown, NY 14701.

Estey Corporation, Drawer E, Red Bank, NJ 07701.

Globe-Wernicke, Cincinnati, OH.

Harvard Interiors Manufacturing Co., Inc., 4820 Durfee Avenue, Pico Rivers, CA 90660.

John E. Sjostrom Co., Inc., 1716 North 10th Street, Philadelphia, PA 19122.

The Worden Company, 199 East 17th Street, Holland, MI 49423.

APPENDIX C

Denominational Services to Libraries

American Baptist Convention
>Write: Department of Leadership Education
>Board of Education and Publication
>Valley Forge, PA 19481

American Lutheran Church
>Write: Lutheran Church Library Association
>122 W. Franklin Avenue
>Minneapolis, MN 55404

Associate Reformed Presbyterian Church
>Write: Book Department
>Associate Reformed Presbyterian Church
>Due West, SC 29639

Christian Church (Disciples of Christ)
>Write: Christian Board of Publication
>Box 179
>St. Louis, MO 63166

Cumberland Presbyterian Church
>Write: Division of Christian Education
>Box 4149
>Memphis, TN 38104

Lutheran Church in America
>Write: Departmental-Field Division
>Board of Parish Education
>2900 Queen Lane
>Philadelphia, PA 19129

Moravian Church in America
>Write: Board of Christian Education and Evangelism
>Moravian Church, North

5 West Market Street
Bethlehem, PA 18010
or
Moravian Church, South
500 South Church Street
Winston-Salem, NC 27101

PRESBYTERIAN CHURCH IN THE U.S.

Write: Church Library Service
Box 1176
Richmond, VA 23209

PROTESTANT EPISCOPAL CHURCH

Write: Seabury Press
815 Second Avenue
New York, NY 10017

REFORMED CHURCH IN AMERICA

Write: Reformed Church Bookstore
811 Palisade Avenue
Teaneck, NJ 07666

SOUTHERN BAPTIST CONVENTION

Write: Church Library Department
Sunday School Board of the
Southern Baptist Convention
127 Ninth Avenue, North
Nashville, TN 37203

UNITED CHURCH OF CHRIST

Write: United Church Board for Homeland Ministries
1505 Race Street
Philadelphia, PA 19102

UNITED METHODIST CHURCH

Write: Church Library Service
201 Eighth Avenue, South
Nashville, TN 37203

UNITED PRESBYTERIAN CHURCH IN THE U.S.A.

Write: Westminster Church Library Plan
Board of Christian Education
Witherspoon Building
Philadelphia, PA 19107

Bibli...

Buder, Christine. ... Press, 1955 (out ...

Church Library M... ... Winona Lake, In...

Hannaford, Claudi... Out." *Spectrum* ...

John, Erwin E. *T...* Augsburg Publish...

Johnson, Marian S. ... apolis: Augsburg Publishing House, 1966.

————. *Promoting Your Church Library.* Minneapolis: Augsburg Publishing House, 1968.

Religious Publishing Houses, compiled by Group Services Librarian, Vigo County Public Library. Terre Haute, Ind.: [1972].

Smith, Ruth S. *Outline for Building Vitality in Your Church Library.* Rev. ed. Washington, D. C.: Church Library Council, [1967].

————. *Workshop Planning.* Guide No. 3. Bryn Mawr, Pa.: Church and Synagogue Library Association, 1972. Part I: Committee and Chairman's Guide. Part II: Group Leader's Guide. Part III: Sample Materials.

Towns, Elmer L., and Barber, Cyril J. *Successful Church Libraries.* Grand Rapids: Baker Book House, 1971.